INDIANS

OF THE NORTHEAST

Edited by Karin Luisa Badt

Women at work in an Iroquois village, pounding corn and carrying firewood. (From a detail on a map by F. G. Bressani, 1657)

Discovery Enterprises, Ltd.
Carlisle, Massachusetts

© Discovery Enterprises, Ltd., Carlisle, MA 1997

ISBN 1-878668-80-3 paperback edition
Library of Congress Catalog Card Number 97-67538

10   9   8   7   6   5   4   3   2   1

Printed in the United States of America

Subject Reference Guide:

Indians of the Northeast
edited by Karin Luisa Badt
Northeast Indians/Native Americans — U.S. History
Six Nations — U.S. History
Indian Reservations — U.S. History
Captivity Narratives — U.S. History

Photos/Illustrations:

Front and back cover:
Details from "Roger Williams being welcomed by the Narragansett Indians," courtesy of the New York Public Library

Other illustrations: Credited where they appear in the book.

Table of Contents

Foreword

Karin Luisa Badt

When the last glimmers of sun blaze in the gloom, filtering through the leaves and casting everything the soil, the bark, the mulching logs in the moss with a dazzling golden sheen, then, at that twilight hour in the forest, one can understand the intensity of life as it was for the Northeastern American Indians so many years ago.

The northeast coast of America — from what is today Canada to New Jersey — was once a wilderness of forests and lakes, marshes and creeks, all humming with life. Deer, elk, bears, wild geese, and wild turkey roamed the woods; blackberries and blueberries ripened on bushes in the summer; fish swam in water as clear as the sky above them. This land was the home to several groups of people, all of whom experienced great joy and thankfulness for the extraordinary beauty of their environment.

Over the tens of thousands of years that these groups lived here, they developed a highly evolved sense of spiritual union with the natural world.

These original northern Americans can be divided into three distinct groups: those who spoke an Iroquoian language, those who spoke an Algonquian language, and those who spoke a Siouan language. Each general language group consisted of numerous distinct tribes, for example, the Huron and Tuontati peoples of the Iroquois group, or the Delaware, Massachuset and Narraganset peoples of the Algonquian group. Some hunted wild game and farmed vegetables, such as squash and

5

corn. Others, along the coast, harvested mussels and lobsters. Yet, while each people developed its own way of life — its own political structure, religious world view, and social codes — they also shared many cultural values and habits.

Oneida family, with the male as a hunter and females caring for the children (1807)

The village was the center of life for most of these peoples, although the kinds of homes they built varied. The Iroquois lived in large bark-covered homes called "longhouses." About ten to twelve families lived in one longhouse, structured in two rows, with each family having its own particular space, and sharing a fire with the family across from them. Thus, a longhouse with ten families would have five campfires running down the center of it. Some Algonquin peoples also lived in longhouses, but many lived in small wigwams, made of bark strips wrapped around a pole. Both the Algonquin and Iroquoian peoples tended to stay in one area for many years, moving only when the necessity for new farmland or hunting grounds inspired them to move on.

American Indians passed down their culture orally, by telling stories. Late at night, the elders of the group would tell stories around the campfire, teaching the young the lessons of many generations of people. One important kind of story for the tribes was the tale which told how the world came to be. In fact, almost every people in the world has its own origin tale; this tale provides a sense of identity.

Iroquois village (Henry E. Huntington Library)

The Creation

Following is an Iroquois tale of creation.

Source: Joseph Bruchac, storyteller, *Iroquois Stories: Heroes and Heroines, Monsters and Magic*. Trumansburg, New York: The Crossing Press. 1985. pp 15-17.

Before this world came to be,
there lived in the Sky-World
an ancient chief.
In the center of his land
grew a beautiful tree
which had four white roots
stretching to each
of the four directions:
North, South, East and West.
From that beautiful tree,
all good things grew.

Then it came to be
that the beautiful tree
was uprooted and through
the hole it made in the Sky-World
fell the youthful wife
of the ancient chief,
a handful of seeds,
which she grabbed from the tree
as she fell, clutched in her hand.

Far below there were only water
and water creatures
who looked up as they swam.

"Someone comes," said the duck
"We must make room for her."

The great turtle swam up
from his place in the depths.
"There is room on my back,"
the great turtle said.

"But there must be earth
where she can stand," said the duck
and so he dove beneath the waters,
but he could not reach the bottom.

"I shall bring up earth,"
the loon then said and he dove too,
but could not reach the bottom.

"I shall try," said the beaver
and he too dove,
but could not reach the bottom.

Finally the muskrat tried.
He dove as deeply as he could,
swimming until his lungs almost burst.
With one paw he touched the bottom,
and came up with a tiny speck
of earth clutched in his paw.

"Place the earth on my back,"
the great turtle said,
and as they spread
the tiny speck of earth it grew

larger and larger and larger
until it became the whole world.

Then two swans flew up
and between their wings
they caught the woman
who fell from the sky.
They brought her gently
down to the earth
where she dropped her handful
of seeds from the Sky-World.

Then it was, that the first plants grew
and life on this new earth began.

World View

The legends of the Northeastern Indians reflect many of their values. For example, common among the Algonquins were tales involving "stars." In these tales, one notices that humans transform into stars or animals, and vice versa. These easy transformations show how close the Algonquins felt towards nature. Not only did they feel that they were part of nature, but they believed that everything in nature had its own spirit and power.

Osseo
or
The Son Of The Evening Star
An Algonquin Tale

Source: Mentor L. Williams, editor. *Schoolcraft's Indian Legends.* East Lansing, Michigan: Michigan State University Press. 1956 pp. 192-195.

There once lived an Indian in the north, who had ten daughters, all of whom grew up to woman-hood. They were noted for their beauty, but especially Oweenee, the youngest, who was very independent in her way of thinking. She...paid very little attention to the numerous young men who came to her father's lodge for the purpose of seeing her....At last she married an old man called Osseo, who was scarcely able to walk, and was too poor to have things like others. They jeered and laughed at her, on all sides, but she seemed to be quite happy....Soon after, the sisters and their husbands and their parents were all invited to a

11

feast, and as they walked along the path, they could not help pitying their young and handsome sister, who had such an unsuitable mate. Osseo often stopped and gazed upwards, but they could perceive nothing in the direction he looked, unless it was the faint glimmering of the evening star....

"Poor old man," said she, "he is talking to his father, what a pity it is, that he would not fall and break his neck, that our sister might have a handsome young husband." Presently they passed a large hollow log, lying with one end, toward the path. The moment Osseo, who was of the turtle totem, came to it, he stopped short, uttered a loud and peculiar yell, and then dashing into one end of the log, he came out at the other, a most beautiful young man, and springing back to the road, he led off the party with steps as light as the reindeer. But on turning round to look for his wife, behold, she had been changed into an old, decrepit woman, who was bent almost double, and walked with a cane. The husband, however, treated her very kindly, as she had done him during the time of his enchantment, and, constantly addressed her by the term of ne-ne-moosh-a, or my sweetheart.

At the wedding feast, Osseo's father began to speak:

"My son-my son," said the voice, "I have seen your afflictions and pity your wants. I come to call you away from a scene that is stained with blood and tears. The earth is full of sorrows...."

"Every night they are lifting their voices to the Power of Evil, and everyday they make themselves busy casting evil in the hunter's path. You have long been their victim, but shall be their victim no more. The spell you were under is broken. ...Ascend, my son, ascend into the skies...."

"The food set before you is enchanted and blessed. Fear not to partake of it. It is endowed with magic power to give immortality to mortals, and to change men to spirits. Your bowls and kettles shall no longer be wood and earth. The one shall become silver and the other wampum. They shall shine like fire, and glisten like the most beautiful scarlet. Every female shall also change her state and looks, and no longer be doomed to laborious tasks. She shall put on the beauty of the starlight, and become a shining bird of the air, clothed with shining feathers. She shall dance and not work — she shall sing and not cry."

"My beams," continued the voice, "shine faintly on your lodge, but they have a power to transform it into the lightness of the skies, and decorate it with the colors of the clouds. Come, Osseo, my son, and dwell no longer on earth...."

Very soon the lodge began to shake and tremble, and they felt it rising into the air. It was too late to run out, for they were already as high as the tops of the trees. Osseo looked around him as the lodge passed through the topmost boughs, and behold! their wooden dishes were changed into shells of a scarlet color, the poles of the lodge to glittering wires of silver, and the bark that covered them into the gorgeous wings of insects. A moment more, and his brothers and sisters, and their parents and friends, were transformed into birds of various plumage....

But Oweenee still kept her earthly garb, and exhibited all the indications of extreme age. He again cast his eyes in the direction of the clouds, and uttered that peculiar yell, which had given him the victory in the hollow log. In a moment the youth and beauty of his wife returned;...The lodge again shook and trembled, for they were now passing through the uppermost clouds, and they immediately after found themselves in the Evening Star, the residence of Osseo's father.

....

Osseo lived happy and contented in the parental lodge, and in due time his wife presented him with a son, who grew up rapidly, and was the image of his father. He was very quick and ready in learning everything that was done in his grandfather's dominions, but he wished also to learn the art of hunting, for he had heard that this was a favorite pursuit below....He soon became expert, and the very first day brought down a bird, but when he went to pick it up, to his amazement, it was a beautiful young woman with the arrow sticking in her breast. It was one of his younger aunts. The moment her blood fell upon the surface of that pure and spotless planet, the charm was dissolved. The boy immediately found himself sinking, but was partly upheld, by something like wings, till he passed through the lower clouds, and he then suddenly dropped upon a high, romantic island in a large lake. He was pleased on looking up, to see all his aunts and uncles following him in the form of birds, and he soon discovercd the silver lodge, with his father and mother, descending with its waving barks looking like so many insects' gilded wings. It rested on the highest cliffs of the island, and here they fixed their residence. They all resumed their natural shapes, but were diminished to the size of fairies, and as a mark of homage to the King of the Evening Star, they never failed on every pleasant evening, during the summer season, to join hands, and dance upon the top of the rocks. These rocks were quickly observed by the Indians to be covered, in moonlight evenings, with a larger sort Of PUK WUDJ ININEES, or little men, and were called Mishin-e-mok-in-ok-ong, or turtle spirits, and the island is named from them to this day. Their shining lodge can be seen in the summer evenings when the moon shines strongly on the pinnacles of the rocks, and the fishermen, who go near those high cliffs at night, have even heard the voices of the happy little dancers.

Dreams

Northeastern American Indians believed dreams were sources of truth. The Iroquois, for example, devoted a lot of time to interpreting the significance of their dreams. They understood that a dream told what it was that a person really needed or desired. It was important to interpret these dreams, because if the person did not get what he or she wanted, unhappiness or sickness would result.

Mohegan Dream Beliefs in the Early Twentieth Century

What follows is an anthropologist's account of the significance of dreams among the Mohegan people.

Source: Glady Tantaquiddgeon, from *Native Tribes and Dialects of Connecticut: A Mohegan-Pequot Diary*. In *Forty-third Annual Report of the Bureau of American Ethnology, 1925-1926*, Washington, D.C.: Government Printing Office. pp. 249-250.

Among the Mohegan there is a belief that dreams are messages from their ancestors who are in the spirit world. These spiritual advisors appear in dreams to guide and instruct the dreamer. Sometimes they bear messages of hope and encouragement and on other occasions warn one of impending danger or death. If a person has the same dream three nights in succession the dream will come true. To prevent its recurrence the dreamer must turn the soles of his shoes upward before retiring at night. Never tell dreams which denote ill luck before breakfast.

Several informants said that they had recurrent dreams and one young woman told the following dream which occurs before or during illness of a relative:

"On Fort Hill, near the ruins of the ancient council seat of Uncas, a blazing fire is seen. A huge pot is suspended over the flame. An Indian, tall and straight, wrapped in a bright-colored blanket and wearing a war bonnet, is stirring the contents of the pot with a long-handled wooden paddle. If the boiling substance rises to the top and flows over the sides the person who is ill dies. If it does not overflow and ceases to boil the person will recover."

Another informant told a recurrent dream in which a black monster with terrible claws and wide spreading wings appears. This is a sign that death will claim one of the tribe within a short time.

Nearly everyone in this group believes that to dream of black animals or objects is an evil omen. To dream of negroes is a sign of trouble and disappointment in the future.

During the past summer a Mohegan woman had a dream in which the spirit of her mother came and told her to tell the people to continue with their plans for the annual wigwam festival. This message inspired the people and with renewed courage they set to work determined to carry out the old custom that it might please the spirits of the departed ones. The affair was a great success.

At the same time, while walking near our burying ground one day, I had the good fortune to pick up a perfect stone ax. Upon showing it to some of my relatives, several of them remarked that it was the spirit of one of my ancestors which led me to the spot where I found the ax. They believed it to be a sign of good luck and to encourage me in my work.

Messages from my brother who is in the spirit world are received quite frequently, by members of the family, in dreams.

To dream of snow and ice denotes good luck. Clear, running water denotes good luck; muddy water, ill luck.

To dream of vermin warns one of illness in the family.

Dreaming of snakes is a sign that you have enemies. If you kill the snake you can overcome your enemies.

Should anyone dream of a snake it is a sign of having an enemy. If on the next day the dreamer should kill a snake he would be able to thwart the evil design. This belief is shared by the Penobscot and their relatives in northern New England.

Political Organization

Sometime in the mid-sixteenth century, five separate Iroquois groups — the Mohawks, Oneidas, Onondagas, Cayugas, and Senecas — decided to form a confederacy. This meant that while each group had its own chief, the chiefs would meet several times each year to agree on decisions for the entire Iroquois Confederacy. In 1715, the League of Five Nations invited a sixth group to join them, the Tuscaroras, and henceforth the Confederacy was referred to as the "Six Nations."

When the founding fathers of the United States Constitution got together in the late eighteenth century to discuss what kind of political organization their new country should have, they were inspired by the Iroquois Confederacy. The Iroquois helped give them the idea that it would be possible to have separate groups of people, each with its own power, with a greater federal power uniting them.

Rites of the Condoling Council

What follows is an excerpt from a chant from an Iroquois ritual, in which the speaker recites the history of the confederacy. This ritual traditionally occurred when one chief died, and another was about to replace him.

Source: A. Grove Day, editor. *The Sky Clears: Poetry of the American Indians.* New York: The Macmillan Company. 1951. pp. 135-140.

Woe! Woe!
Hearken ye!
We are diminished!

Woe! Woe!
The cleared land has become a thicket.
Woe! Woe!
The clear places are deserted.
Woe!
They are in their graves —
They who established it —
Woe!
The great League —
Yet they declared
It should endure —
The great League.
Woe!
Their work has grown old.
Woe!
Thus we are become miserable.

The Caniengas!
Continue to listen!
Thou who wert ruler,
    He-Who-Seeks-the-Wampum-Belt!
    [*Hiawatha*]
That was the roll of you,
You who were joined in the work,
You who completed the work,
The Great League.

....

These were his uncles [the
Onondagas]:
Now hearken!
Thou who wert ruler,
    Entangled One!
Continue to listen!
These were the cousins:
Thou who wert ruler,
    Best-Soil-Uppermost!
Continue to listen!

....

This befell
In ancient times,
They had their children,
Those the two clans.
He the high chief
    Hatchet-in-His-Belt!

This put away the clouds:
He was a war chief;
He was a high chief —
Acting, in either office:
    [name translated]
This was the roll of you!

....

Then, in later times,
They made additions
To the great mansion.
These were at the doorway,

....

They who were cousins,
These two guarded the doorway:
    Tangled Hair!
With his cousin,
    Open Door!
This was the roll of you!

Now we are dejected
In our minds.

Encounter with the Europeans

Delaware Indians' Perception of the Dutch

Europeans arrived on the northeast shore in the 1500s, and, in the beginning, established a friendly trade relationship with the Native Americans. The following is an account of how the Delawares perceived the first arrival of the white man to Manhattan island. (The spelling and grammar have not been altered, and the notes in parentheses are as they originally appeared in all excerpts in this chapter.)

Source: *Indian Tradition of the First Arrival of the Dutch at Manhattan as Related to John Heckwelder*, New York Historical Society Collection, 2nd. Series, I, pp. 71-74. c. 1765.

The following account of the *first* arrival of Europeans at York Island, is verbatim as it was related to me by aged and respected Delawares, Momeys and Mahicanni, (otherwise called Mohigans, Mahicanders,) near forty years ago. It is copied from notes and manuscripts taken on the spot. They say:

A long time ago, when there was no such thing known to the Indians as people with a *white skin*, (their expression,) some Indians who had been out a-fishing, and where the sea widens, espied at a great distance something remarkably large swimming, or floating on the water, and such as they had never seen before. They immediately returning to the shore apprised their countrymen of what they had seen, and pressed them to go out with them and discover what it might be. These together hurried out, and saw to their great surprise the phenomenon, but could not agree what it might be; some concluding it either to be an uncommon large fish, or other animal, while others were of opinion it must be some very large house. It was at length agreed among those who were spectators, that as this phenomenon moved towards the land, whether or not it was an animal, or anything that had life in it, it would be well to inform all the Indians on the inhabited islands of what they had seen, and put them on their guard. Accordingly, they sent runners and watermen off to carry the news to their scattered chiefs, that these might send off in every direction for the warriors to come in. These arriving in numbers, and themselves viewing the strange appearance, and that it was actually moving towards them, (the entrance of the river or bay,) concluded it to be a large canoe or house, in which the great Mannitto (great or Supreme Being) himself was, and that he probably was coming to visit them. By this time the chiefs of the different tribes were assembled on York Island, and were counselling (or deliberating) on the manner they should receive their Mannitto on his arrival. Every step had been taken to be well provided with a plenty of meat for a sacrifice; the women were required to prepare the best of victuals; idols or images were examined and put in order; and a grand dance was supposed not only to be an agreeable entertainment for the Mannitto, but might, with the addition of a sacrifice, contribute towards appeasing him, in case he was angry with them. The conjurors were also set to work, to determine what the meaning of this phenomenon was, and what the result would be. Both to these, and to the chiefs and wise men of the nation, men, women, and children were looking up for advice and protection. Between hope and fear, and in confusion, a dance commenced. While in this situation fresh runners arrive declaring it a house of various colours, and crowded with living creatures. It now appears to be certain that it is the great Mannitto bringing them some kind of game, such as they had not before; but other runners soon after arriving, declare it a large house of various colours, full of people, yet of quite a different colour than they (the Indians) are of; that they were also dressed in a different manner from them, and that one in particular appeared altogether red, which must be the Mannitto himself. They are soon hailed from the vessel, though in a language they do not understand; yet they shout (or yell) in their way. Many are for running off to the woods, but are pressed by others to stay, in order not to give offence to their visiters, who could find them out, and might destroy them. The house (or large canoe, as some will have it,) stops, and a smaller canoe comes ashore with the red man and some others in it; some stay by this canoe to guard it. The chiefs and wise men (or councillors) had composed a large circle, unto which the red-clothed man with two others approach. He salutes them with friendly countenance, and they return the salute after their manner. They are lost in admiration, both as to the colour of the skin (or these whites) as also to their manner of dress, yet most as to the habit of him who wore the red clothes, which shone with something they could not account for. He must be the great Mannitto (Supreme Being,) they think, but why should he have a *white skin*? A large hockhack [Their word for gourd, bottle, decanter] is brought forward by one of the (supposed) Mannitto's servants, and from this a substance is poured out into a small cup (or glass) and handed to the Mannitto. The (expected) Mannitto drinks; has the glass filled again, and hands it to the chief next to him to drink. The chief receives the glass, but only smelleth at it, and passes it on to the next chief, who does the same. The glass thus

24

passes through the circle without the contents being tasted by any one; and is upon the point of being returned again to the red-clothed man, when one of their number, a spirited man and great warrior jumps up — harangues the assembly on the impropriety of returning the glass with the contents in it; that the same was handed them by the Mannitto in order that they should drink it, as he himself had done before them; that this would please him; but to return what he had given to them might provoke him, and be the cause of their being destroyed by him. And that, since he believed it for the good of the nation that the contents offered them *should* be drank, and as no one was willing to drink it he *would*, let the consequence be what it would; and that it was better for one man to die, than a whole nation to be destroyed. He then took the glass and bidding the assembly a farewell, *drank it off*. Every eye was fixed on their resolute companion to see what an effect this would have upon him, and he soon beginning to stagger about, and at last dropping to the ground, they bemoan him. He falls into a sleep, and they view him as expiring. He awakes again, jumps up, and declares that he never felt himself before so happy as after he had drank the cup. Wishes for more. His wish is granted; and the whole assembly soon join him, and become intoxicated. [The Delawares call this place (New-York Island) Mannahattanink or *Mannahachtanink* to this day, They have frequently told me that it derived its name from this general *intoxication*, and that the word comprehended the same as to say, *the island or place of general intoxication*. The Mahicanni, (otherwise called Mohiggans by the English, and Mahicanders by the Low Dutch,) call this place by the same name as the Delawares do; yet think it is owing or given in consequence of a kind of wood which grew there, and of which the Indians used to make their bows and arrows. This wood the latter (Mohiccani) call *"gawaak."* The universal name the Monseys have for New-York, is *Laaphawachking*, which is interpreted, *the place of stringing beads* (wampum). They say this name was given in consequence of beads being here distributed among them by the Europeans; and that after the European vessel had returned, wherever one looked, one would see the Indians employed in stringing the beads or wampum the whites had given them.

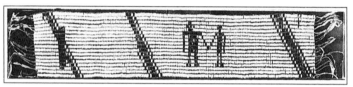

Delaware wampum beads, showing Indian and white man holding hands. This was given to the Quakers, as a symbol of friendship. (National Archives)

After this general intoxication had ceased, (during which time the whites had confined themselves to their vessel,) the man with the red clothes returned again to them, and distributed presents among them, to wit, beads, axes, hoes, stockings, &c. They say that they had become familiar to each other, and were made to understand by signs; that they now would return home, but would visit them next year again, when they would bring them more presents, and stay with them awhile; but that, as they could not live without eating, they should then want a little land of them to sow some seeds in order to raise herbs to put in their broth. That the vessel arrived the season following, and they were much rejoiced at seeing each other; but that the whites laughed at them (the Indians,) seeing they knew not the use of the axes, hoes, &c., they had given them, they having had these hanging to their breasts as ornaments; and the stockings they had made use of as tobacco pouches. The whites now put handles (or helves) in the former, and cut trees down before their eyes, and dug the ground, and showed them the use of the stockings. Here (say they) a general laughter ensued, among them (the Indians), that they had remained for so long a time ignorant of the use of so valuable implements; and had borne with the weight of such heavy metal hanging to their necks for such a length of time. They took every white man they saw for a Mannitto, yet inferior and attendant to the *supreme Mannitto*, to wit, to the one which wore the red and laced clothes. Familiarity daily increasing between them and the whites, the latter now proposed to stay with them, asking them only for so much land as the hide of a bullock would cover (or encompass,) which hide was brought forward and spread on the ground before them. That they readily granted this request; whereupon the whites took a knife, and beginning at one place on this hide, cut it up into a rope not thicker than the finger of a little child, so that by the time this hide was cut up there was a great heap. That this rope was drawn out to a great distance, and then brought round again, so that both ends might meet. That they carefully avoided its breaking, and that upon the whole it encompassed a large piece of ground. That they (the Indians) were surprised at the superior wit of the whites, but did not wish to contend with them about a little land, as they had enough. That they and the whites lived for a long time contentedly together, although these asked from time to time more land of them; and proceeding higher up the Mahicanittuk (Hudson river), they believed they would soon want all their country, and which at this time was already the case.

[Here ends this relation.]

Puritans Encounter the American Indian

In 1620, a group of English people, seeking religious freedom, crossed the Atlantic and established a colony in what is today Massachusetts. William Bradford became governor of this colony, and in his journal, he describes his impressions of the first "Indians" he met. These American Indians were responsible for the survival of the early colonists. With the help of an Algonquin named Squanto, the Pilgrims learned how to farm native vegetables, such as pumpkin and corn, in order to survive in their new, and often harsh, environment. A detailed account of life in early Plymouth may be found in Of Plymouth Plantation, 1620-1647, by William Bradford, Sometime Governor Thereof. *Passages of special interest are excerpted in* Faith Unfurled: The Pilgrims' Quest for Freedom *in this* Perspectives on History Series *from Discovery Enterprises, Ltd.*

The Purchase of Manhattan

While the English Puritans established colonies up north, the Dutch settled along the Hudson river, in what is today New York City and northern New Jersey. The Dutch and English had different approaches to the American Indian. While the English tended not to respect the Indian's claim to their land, the Dutch considered the native Americans to be the rightful owners of their territory. Thus, they made treaties with the American Indians in order to buy their land from them and to establish trade agreements.

These treaties, however, often exploited the Indians, as one can see in the following description of the purchase of Manhattan island.

[November 5, 1626]

High and Mighty Lords:

Yesterday, arrived here the Ship the Arms of Amsterdam, which sailed from New Netherland, out of the River Mauritius, on the 23rd September. They report that our people are in good heart and live in peace there; the Women also have borne some children there. They have purchased the Island Manhattes from the Indians for the value of 60 guilders; 'tis 11,000 morgens in size. They had all their grain sowed by the middle of May, and reaped by the middle of August. They send thence samples of summer grain; such as wheat, rye, barley, oats, buck-wheat, canary seed, beans and flax.

The cargo of the aforesaid ship is:

> 7246 Beaver skins.
>
> 178 1/2 Otter skins.
>
> 675 Otter skins.
>
> 48 Minck skins.
>
> 36 Wild cat skins.
>
> 33 Mincks.
>
> 34 Rat skins.
>
> Considerable Oak timber and Hickory.

Herewith, High and Mighty Lords, be commended to the mercy of the Almighty.

[Endorsed]
In Amsterdam, the 5th November, 1626.
Received 7th November, 1626.

[Addressed]
High and Mighty Lords,
My Lords the States General at the Hague

> Your High Mightinesses' obedient,
> (Signed) P. Schagen.

Complaints of the Esopus

The relationship between the Dutch and the American Indians soon became full of tension. Skirmishes between the two peoples became frequent, and resulted in war. Below is a European account of the complaints made by the Esopus Indians against Dutch treatment.

[September 4, 1659]

The *Esopus* Indians, numbering about 96, small and large all told, made the following propositions on the 4th of September.

First; that on the 3rd of September thay had been together at one of their savage houses and only deliberated upon good things, as they now proved coming with women and children and without arms, so that we might not have any suspicion of them.

Second, that two *Mingaes Sachems*, *Sinnekens* and southern Indians had been with them and had advised, that they should reconcile themselves again with the Christians, for which purpose they had now come: they had also said, they should be ashamed to act so toward the Christians.

Third, three years ago last fall they had been at the Manhatans, then they came here to the *Esopus*, but they did not injure any one of the *Dutch* nor did any other harm and they let the Christians return to their possessions and shortly after they made an everlasting compact with the Christians and the *Maquaes* and to confirm it, they locked their arms together with iron chains and said, who shall first break this, he shall be made war against in common.

Fourth, that they altogether willing to be peaceful and had no more evil intentions, people may go to work now, as one fire is burning between us and we may go to sleep on either side with safety and that formerly many news reports had come from other savages, that the *Dutch* would come to kill them, and then this and that, but that now they would not listen to such talk.

Fifth, that they cannot understand, why the Fort had been made here; that it would have been better, if every one had remained on his bouwery, for then we Christians would have been enabled to harvest our corn better, while now it is spoiled and the horses would have brought home more in one day, than what now has been carried off by the water.

Sixth, that they have been wondering, why we do not plough; they had suspected us of evil intentions, but we should commence ploughing, whereas we need not fear any harm from them and that they are not very well pleased, because they can not use the path, which formerly run through the guardhouse-grounds; that it was lucky, that the soldiers had beaten just a Sachem or some others, for using that path, for if it had been barebacks, they would have lustily fought for it.

Seventh, they say, that *Jacob's* horses and hogs had destroyed a whole plantation and they guess, that, when they drove out the animals, the horse, which *Jacob* lost, must have fallen on a stump, for if it had been shot with a bullet or an arrow, the bullet or arrow-stick would have been found and they say, it died from the cutting open.

Eighth, they brought wampum for the horse and acknowledged, that they had killed it; 40 strings of white wampum.

Ninth, they bring wampum for *Jacob Jansen's* hogs and acknowledge, they had killed them too; 10 strings.

Tenth, Wampum for capturing our four Christians; 3 strings.

Eleventh, Wampum, that we should declare ourselves satisfied; 5 strings.

Twelfth, Wampum, that the soldiers shall not beat them any more; 5 strings.

Twelfth, 32 Wampum, that the *Dutch* shall pay the savages, who have worked for them; 5 strings.

And we have answered, that we could not do anything, but that all would be arranged properly, when his Honor, the General, came. Your Honor will please, to send also an order, what we shall do with the wampum.

Captivity Narratives

The Deerfield Massacre

Native American tribes sometimes joined forces with warring European factions to remove colonists from lands the Indians wanted. In February of 1704, Indians — with the help of French soldiers — attacked the town of Deerfield, Massachusetts, slaughtering about fifty men, women, and children. Over one hundred captives were taken, and most of the town was burned to the ground.

The attack on Indian House, Deerfield, Massachusetts
(Woodcut by Alexander Anderson)

Mary Jemison Becomes an Iroquois

Native American tribes occasionally took revenge against European invasion of their territory, and would capture colonists. Instead of killing their captives, often the Indians would adopt the white person into their community. Some European captives lived for years among the Indians, fully integrated in the culture.

Many of the captivity narratives tell gruesome tales of hard work, separation, and even torture. The excerpt from the narrative of Mary Jemison which follows, tells of her peaceful integration into Iroquios life. Mary was captured at the age of fifteen, in 1758, and lived with the Indians as a family member until her death, at the age of ninety. Her autobiography was published in 1824.

The Captives, by F. O. C. Darley

Source: Found in Peter Nabakov, editor. "Mary Jemison Becomes an Iroquois," *Native American Testimony:An Anthology of Indian and White Relations, First Encounter to Dispossession.* New York: Thomas Y. Crowell, 1978. pp. 90-95.

...Having made fast to the shore, the squaws left me in the canoe while they went to their wigwam or house in the town, and returned with a suit of Indian clothing, all new, and very clean and nice. My clothes, though whole and good when I was taken, were now torn in pieces, so that I was almost naked. They first undressed me and threw my rags into the river; then washed me clean and dressed me in the new suit they had just brought, in complete Indian style; and then led me home and seated me in the center of their wigwam.

I had been in that situation but a few minutes, before all the squaws in the town came in to see me. I was soon surrounded by them, and they immediately set up a most dismal howling, crying bitterly, and wringing their hands in all the agonies of grief for a deceased relative.

Their tears flowed freely, and they exhibited all the signs of real mourning. At the commencement of this scene, one of their number began, in a voice somewhat between speaking and singing, to recite some words to the following purport, and continued the recitation till the ceremony was ended; the company at the same time varying the appearance of their countenances, gestures and tone of voice, so as to correspond with the sentiments expressed by their leader:

"Oh, our brother! Alas! He is dead — he has gone — he will never return! Friendless he died on the field of the slain, where his bones are yet lying unburied! Oh, who will not mourn his sad fate? No tears dropped around him; oh, no! No tears of his sisters were there! He fell in his prime, when his arm was most needed to keep us from danger! Alas! he has gone! and left us in sorrow, his loss to bewail: Oh, where is his spirit?...His spirit has seen our distress, and sent us a helper whom with pleasure we greet. Dickewamis has come: then let us receive her with joy! She is handsome and pleasant! Oh! she is our sister, and gladly we welcome her here. In the place of our brother she stands in our tribe. With care we will guard her from trouble; and may she be happy till her spirit shall leave us."

In the course of that ceremony, from mourning they became serene — joy sparkled in their countenances, and they seemed to rejoice over me as over a long-lost child. I was made welcome amongst them as a sister to the two squaws before mentioned, and was called Dickewamis; which being interpreted, signifies a pretty girl, a handsome girl, or a pleasant, good thing. That is the name by which I have ever since been called by the Indians.

I afterwards learned that the ceremony I at that time passed through, was that of adoption. The two squaws had lost a brother in Washington's war, sometime in the year before, and in consequence of his death went up to Fort Pitt, on the day on which I arrived there, in order to receive a prisoner or an enemy's scalp, to supply their loss....

It was my happy lot to be accepted for adoption; and at the time of the ceremony I was received by the two squaws, to supply the place of their brother in the family; and I was ever considered and treated by them as a real sister, the same as though I had been born of their mother.

During my adoption, I sat motionless, nearly terrified to death at the appearance and actions of the company, expecting every moment to feel their vengeance, and suffer death on the spot. I was, however, happily disappointed, when at the close of the ceremony the company retired, and my sisters went about employing every means for my consolation and comfort.

Being now settled and provided with a home, I was employed in nursing the children, and doing light work about the house. Occasionally I was sent out with the Indian hunters, when they went but a short distance, to help them carry their game. My situation was easy; I had no particular hardships to endure. But still, the recollection of my parents, my brothers and sisters, my home, and my own captivity, destroyed my happiness, and made me constantly solitary, lonesome and gloomy.

My sisters would not allow me to speak English in their hearing; but remembering the charge that my dear mother gave me at the time I left her, whenever I chanced to be alone I made a business of repeating my prayer, catechism, or something I had learned in order that I might not forget my own language. By practising in that way I retained it till I came to Genesee flats, where I soon became acquainted with English people with whom I have been almost daily in the habit of conversing.

My sisters were diligent in teaching me their language; and to their great satisfaction I soon learned so that I could understand it readily, and speak it fluently. I was very fortunate in falling into their hands; for they were kind good natured women; peaceable and mild in their dispositions; temperate and decent in their habits, and very tender and gentle towards me. I have great reason to respect them, though they have been dead a great number of years.

The town where they lived was pleasantly situated on the Ohio, at the mouth of the Shenanjee; the land produced good corn; the woods furnished plenty of game, and the waters abounded with fish. Another river emptied itself into the Ohio, directly opposite the mouth of the Shenanjee. We spent the summer at that place, where we planted, hoed, and harvested a large crop of corn, of an excellent quality....

The corn being harvested, the Indians took it on horses and in canoes, and proceeded down the Ohio, occasionally stopping to hunt a few days, till we arrived at the mouth of Sciota river; where they established their winter quarters, and continued hunting till the ensuing spring, in the adjacent wilderness. While at that place I went with the other children to assist the hunters to bring in their game. The forests on the Sciota were well stocked with elk, deer, and other large animals; and the marshes contained large numbers of beaver, muskrat, etc., which made excellent hunting for the Indians, who depended, for their meat, upon their success in taking elk and deer; and for ammunition and clothing, upon the beaver, muskrat, and other furs that they could take in addition to their peltry.

The season for hunting being passed, we all returned in the spring to the mouth of the river Shenanjee, to the houses and fields we had left in the fall before. There we again planted our corn, squashes, and beans, on the fields that we occupied the preceding summer.

About planting time, our Indians all went up to Fort Pitt, to make peace with the British, and took me with them. We landed on the opposite side of the river from the fort, and encamped for the night. Early the next morning the Indians took me over to the fort to see the white people that were there. It was then that my heart bounded to be liberated from the Indians and to be restored to my friends and my country. The white people were surprised to see me with the Indians, enduring the hardships of a savage life, at so early an age, and with so delicate a constitution as I appeared to possess. They asked me my name; where and when I was taken — and appeared very much interested on my behalf. They were continuing their inquiries, when my sisters became alarmed, believing that I should be taken from them, hurried me into their canoe and recrossed the

Artist Benjamin West portrays a captive child clinging to his Indian mother when a white man comes to take him back to his biological mother. (New York Public Library)

river — took their bread out of the fire and fled with me, without stopping, till they arrived at the river Shenanjee. So great was their fear of losing me, or of my being given up in the treaty, that they never once stopped rowing till they got home.

Shortly after we left the shore opposite the fort, as I was informed by one of my Indian brothers, the white people came over to take me back; but after considerable inquiry, and having made diligent search to find where I was hid, they returned with heavy hearts. Although I had then been with the Indians something over a year, and had become considerably habituated to their mode of living, and attached to my sisters, the sight of white people who could speak English inspired me with an unspeakable anxiety to go home with them, and share in the blessings of civilization. My sudden departure and escape from them, seemed like a second captivity, and for a long time I brooded the thoughts of my miserable situation with almost as much sorrow and dejection as I had done those of my first sufferings. Time, the destroyer of every affection, wore away my unpleasant feelings, and I became as contented as before....

Not long after the Delawares came to live with us [during the first summer], my sisters told me that I must go and live with one of them, whose name was Sheninjee. Not daring to cross them, or disobey their commands, with a great degree of reluctance I went; and Sheninjee and I were married according to Indian custom.

Sheninjee was a noble man; large in stature; elegant in his appearance; generous in his conduct; courageous in war; a friend to peace, and a great lover of justice. He supported a degree of dignity far above his rank, and merited and received the confidence and friendship of all the tribes with whom he was acquainted. Yet, Sheninjee was an Indian. The idea of spending my days with him, at first seemed perfectly irreconcilable to my feelings: but his good nature, generosity, tenderness, and friendship towards me, soon gained my affection; and, strange as it may seem, I loved him! To me he was ever kind in sickness, and always treated me with gentleness; in fact, he was an agreeable husband, and a comfortable companion. We lived happily together till the time of our final separation, which happened two or three years after our marriage, as I shall presently relate....

New Power Alliances

With the arrival of the Europeans, American Indians had to change their relationships with each other. Several Indian nations chose to create alliances with a European power, in order to increase their own status when fighting their traditional enemies. For example, some Long Island Indians made an alliance with the Dutch to fight the Esopus.

The European powers also fought amongst themselves to establish control over what they termed "the new world." Throughout the seventeenth and eighteenth centuries, many skirmishes occurred between the French, English, and Dutch over land. American Indians adapted to this bellicose situation, and often formed alliances with one European group against another, hoping in this way to protect their own position.

Following is an account by Pontiac, a Delaware, explaining his reasons for making an alliance with the French against the English.

Pontiac Makes an Alliance

Source: Wayne Moquin, editor. *Great Documents in American Indian History.* New York: Praeger Publishers. 1973. pp. 124-125.

My brothers, we have never had in view to do you any evil. We have never intended that any should be done you. But amongst my young men there are, as amongst you, some who, in spite of all precautions which we take, always do evil. Besides, it is not only for my revenge that I make war upon the English, it is for you my brothers, as for us. When the English, in their councils, which we have held with them, have insulted us,

41

they have also insulted you, without your knowing anything about it, and as: I know all our brothers know, the English have taken from you all means of avenging yourselves, by disarming you and making you write on a paper, which they have sent to their country, which they could not make us do; therefore, I will avenge you equally with us, and I swear their annihilation as long as any of them shall remain on our land. Besides, you do not know all the reasons which oblige me to act as I do. I have told you only that which regards you. You will know the rest in time. I know well that I pass amongst many of my brothers for a fool, but you will see in the future if I am such as is said, and if I am wrong. I also know well that there are amongst you, my brothers, some who take the part of the English, to make war against us, and that only pains me on their account. I know them well, and when our father shall have come, I will name them and point them out to him, and they will see whether they or we shall be the most content in the future.

Iroquois and British battle the French (National Archives)

I doubt not, my brothers, that this war tries you, on account of the movements of our brothers, who all the time go and come to your houses. I am sorry for it but do not believe, my brothers, that I instigate the wrong which is done to you, and for proof that I do not wish it, remember the war of the Foxes, and the manner in which I have behaved in your interest. It is now seventeen years that the Sauteux and Ottawas of Michelimakinak and all the nations of the north have come with the Takes [Sacs] and Foxes to annihilate you. Who has defended you? Was it not I and my people? When Mekinak, great chief of all the nations, said in his council that he would carry to his village the head of your commander, and eat his heart and drink his blood, have I not taken up your interest by going to his camp and telling him, if he wanted to kill the French, he must commence with me and my people? Have I not helped you to defeat them and drive them away? When or how came that? Would you, my brothers, believe that I to-day would turn my arms against you? No, my brothers, I am the same French Pondiak who lent you his hand seventeen years ago. I am a Frenchman, and I want to die a Frenchman! And I repeat to you they are both your interests and mine which I revenge. Let me go on. I don't ask your assistance, because I know you cannot give it. I only ask of you Provisions for me and all my people. If, however, you would like to aid me, I would not refuse you. You would cause me pleasure, and you would the sooner be out of trouble. For I warrant you, when the English shall be driven from here or killed, we shall all retire to our villages according to our custom, and await the arrival of our father, the Frenchman. These, you see, my brothers, are my sentiments. Rest assured, my brothers, I will watch that no more wrong shall be done to you by my people, nor by other Indians. What I ask of you is that our women be allowed to plant our corn on the fallows [clearings] of your lands. We shall be obliged to you for that.

43

The Decline of Power

When the United States became a nation, Native Americans realized that they, like the British and French, had lost their claim to equal nationhood on the American continent. Before, during the Revolutionary War, some American Indian peoples had sided with the colonists, others with the British. But afterwards they no longer had allies to protect their position, and found themselves forced to give up land to the new Americans.

Below is an account by a Seneca leader, asking President George Washington to restore land taken from the Iroquois Confederacy during the Revolutionary War.

The Seneca Nation Speaks

Source: Original document found in T.C. McLuhan, *Touch the Earth: A Self-Portrait of Indian Existence*. New York: Outerbridge & Dienstfrey, pp. 131, 133.

FATHER! The voice of the Seneca nation speaks to you, the Great Counsellor, in whose heart the wise men of all the thirteen fires [thirteen states], have placed their wisdom. What we may have to say may appear small in your ears and we therefore entreat you to hearken with attention, for we are about to speak of things of very great importance.

When your army entered the country of the Six Nations we called you the TOWN DESTROYER, and to this day, when that terrible name is heard, our women look behind and turn pale, and our children cling to the breasts of their mothers.

Chief Cornplanter

Our Counsellors and Warriors are men, and cannot be afraid, but their hearts are grieved on account of the distress of our women and children.

[Cornplant then set forth in detail the stratagems and other iniquitous means that had been used to deceive the Indians, compelling them to surrender the great country lately given up. He referred to the part he had himself been led to take in making the treaty, describing the effect produced on the minds of his people towards him.]

Father! When that great country was surrendered, there were but few Chiefs present, and they were compelled to give it up and it is not the Six Nations only that reproach these Chiefs with having giv[en] up that country; the Chippewas, and all the Nations who lived on those Lands, westward, call to us and ask us, "brothers of our fathers, where is the place you have reserved for us to lie down upon?"

Father! you have compelled us to do that which has made us ashamed. We have nothing to answer to the children of the brothers of our fathers. When, last Spring, they called upon us to go to war, to secure a bed to lie upon, the Senecas entreated them to be quiet, until we had spoken to you....

Father! we will not conceal from you, that the Great God, and not man, has preserved Cornplant from the hands of his own Nation; for they ask continually: "where is the Land which our children, and their children after them are to lie upon?" You told us, they say, "that the line drawn from Pennsylvania to Lake Ontario, would mark it forever or, the East; and the line running from Beaver Creek to Pennsylvania, would mark it on the West, and we see that it is not so. For first one, and then another, comes and takes it away, by order of that people which you tell us promised to secure it to us." He is silent, for he has nothing to answer. When the Sun goes down, he opens his heart before his God, and earlier than the Sun appears upon the hills, he gives thanks for his protection during the night; for he feels that among men, made desperate by their wrongs, it is God alone that can preserve him. He loves peace, and all that he had in store he has given to those who have been robbed by your people, lest they should plunder the innocent to repay themselves. The whole season, while others have been employed in providing for their families, he has spent in his endeavors to preserve peace, and at this moment his wife and children are lying on the ground, and in want of food; his heart is pained for them, but he perceives that the Great God will try his firmness in doing what is right.

Father! you have said we are in your hand, and that by shutting it you could crush us to nothing. Are you determined to crush us?...

Father! innocent men of our Nation are killed, one after another, and of our best families, but none of your people who have committed these murders have been punished. We now ask you, was it intended that your people should kill the Senecas, and not only remain unpunished by you, but be protected by you against the revenge of the next of kin?

Father! these are to us very great things. We know that you are very strong we have heard you are wise — and we now wait to receive your answer to what we have said, that we may know if you are just.

Reservations

The United States made treaties with several American Indian nations, agreeing to allow them limited areas of land, called reservations, in exchange for peace. The following is the 1794 Treaty made with the Iroquois Confederacy.

Treaty with the Six Nations, November 11, 1794

ARTICLE I

Peace and friendship are hereby firmly established, and shall be perpetual, between the United States and the Six Nations.

ARTICLE II

The United States acknowledge the lands reserved to the Oneida, Onondaga and Cayuga Nations, in their respective treaties with the state of New York, and called their reservations, to be their property; and the United States will never claim the same, nor disturb them or either of the Six Nations, nor their Indian friends residing thereon and united with them, in the free use of enjoyment thereof: but the said reservations shall remain theirs, until they choose to sell the same to the people of the United States who have right to purchase.

ARTICLE III

The land of the Seneka nation is bounded as folows: [description follows]. Now, the United States acknowledge all the land within the aforementioned boundaries, to be the property of the Seneka nation; and the United States will never claim the same, nor disturb the Seneka nation, nor any of the Six Nations, or their Indian friends residing thereon and united with them, in the free use and enjoyment thereof: but it shall remain theirs, until they choose to sell the same to the people of the United States, who have the right to purchase.

ARTICLE IV

The United States having thus described and acknowledged what lands belong to the Oneidas, Onondagas, Cayugas and Senekas, and engaged never to claim the same, nor to disturb them, or any of the Six Nations, or their Indian friends residing thereon and united with them, in the free use and enjoyment thereof: Now the Six Nations, and each of them, hereby engage that they will never claim any other lands within the boundaries of the United States; nor ever disturb the pcople of the United States in the free use and enjoyment thereof.

....

ARTICLE VII

Lest the firm peace and friendship now established should be interrupted by the misconduct of individuals, the United States and Six Nations agree, that for injuries done by individuals on either side, no private revenge or retaliation shall take place; but, instead thereof, complaint shall be made by the party injured, to the other: By the Six Nations or any of them, to the President of the United States, or the Superintendent by him appointed: and by the Superintendent, or other person appointed by the President, to the principal chiefs of the Six Nations, or of the nation to which the offender belongs: and such prudent measures shall then be pursued as shall be necessary to preserve our peace and friendship unbroken; until the legislature (or great council) of the United States shall make the equitable provision for the purpose.

Indian Removal

Reservations were only a short-term solution. The United States decided it did not want to co-exist with the Indian nations. Thus in 1825, President James Monroe proposed the "Indian Removal Act," which would force tribes to move out West, to what was considered uninhabitable land. Tens of thousands of Northeast Indians had to abandon their homelands, and move to reservations out West. Thousands died on the journey.

James Monroe on Indian Removal

Below is President Monroe's justification for Indian Removal. Note that he takes the position that Indian Removal is for the "benefit" of the Indians themselves.

Source: Original document by James Monroe, a message to Congress in 1825. Found in Edward H. Spicer, *A Short History of the Indians of the United States.* New York: D. Van Nostrand Company. 1969. pp. 229-230.

Being deeply impressed with the opinion, that the removal of the Indian tribes from the lands which they now occupy within the limits of the several States and Territories, to the country lying westward and northward thereof, within our own acknowledged boundaries, is of very high importance to our Union, and may be accomplished on conditions, and in a manner, to promote the interest and happiness of those tribes, the attention has long been drawn, with great solicitude, to the object. For the removal of the tribes within the State of

Georgia, the motive has been peculiarly strong, arising from the compact with that State, whereby the United States are bound to extinguish the Indian title to the lands within it, whenever it may be done peaceably and on reasonable conditions. In the fufilment of this compact I have thought that the United States should act with a generous spirit, that they should omit nothing which should comport with a liberal construction of the instrument, and likewise be in accordance with the just rights of these tribes. From the view which I have taken of the subject, I am satisfied that, in the discharge of those important duties, in regard to both the parties alluded to, the United States will have to encounter no conflicting interests with either; on the contrary, that the removal of the tribes, from territory which they now inhabit, to that which was designated in the message at the commencement of the session, which would accomplish the object for Georgia, under a well digested plan for their government and civilization, which should be agreeable to themselves, would not only shield them from impending ruin, but promote their welfare and happiness. Experience has clearly demonstrated, that in their present state, it is impossible to incorporate them, in such masses, in any form whatever, into our system. It has also demonstrated, with equal certainty, that, without a timely anticipation of, and provision against, the dangers to which they are exposed, under causes which it will be difficult, if not impossible, to control, their degradation and extermination will be inevitable....

To the United States, the proposed arrangement offers many advantages in addition to those which have been already enumerated. By the establishment of such a government over these tribes, with their consent, we become, in reality their benefactors. The relation of conflicting interests, which has heretofore existed between them and our frontier settlements, will cease. There will be no more war between them and the United States. Adopting such a government, their movement will be in harmony with us, and its good effect be felt throughout the whole extent of our territory, to the Pacific. It may fairly be presumed, that, through the agency of such a government, the Condition of all the tribes inhabiting that vast region may be essentially improved; that permanent peace may be preserved with them and our commerce be much extended.

Native American Protest

Despite the many obstacles, Native American cultures have contin-
ued to thrive up to the present day. The twentieth century became the
time for many Indian groups to assert their rights. They demanded
that the United States government redress the wrongs which it com-
mitted in its severe take-over of the American continent.

As the following account by Peter Blue Cloud demonstrates,
struggles over property persist until the present day, in both the
United States and Canada. The Canadian town of Oka wished to
violate a treaty with the Iroquois, and use its land for a golf course.
The Iroquois Mohawks protested.

An Account by Peter Blue Cloud

Source: *Native American Testimony: A Chronicle of Indian-White Relations from Proph-*
ecy to the Present, 1492-1992. New York: Viking Penguin. 1991. pp. 433-435.

Day 70. 18 September 1990.

A light ground frost shimmers the grass. Bright stars poke in
and out of clouds. I sit in darkness, sipping coffee and thinking
of the coming winter. It is time to pick the remaining foods in
the garden. As on other mornings in the past few weeks, I try
to think of things unrelated to the presence of the Canadian
Army surrounding our lands. I am very tired of being a hostage
to Canada. I want it to end soon. Why doesn't the government negotiate as they promised?

I am sitting on my porch above the very beach where I

learned to swim and to fish as a child, remembering when violence and death were dreamlike happenings in a World War far away — the only visible evidence, back then, in the many uniformed men walking our roads to visit relatives for that final good-bye.

....

The people of Kahnawake, unarmed, crossed the bridge and confronted automatic-weapons-carrying troops. There was no fear on the faces of our Mohawk people, only anger. The Army quickly grouped, weapons at the ready, and ready, too, to say, "We were only following orders." "Get off our land!" was the main cry of the people, nose to nose with those apprehensive-looking soldiers. As the crowd grew and pushed into the line of soldiers, the first barrage of tear gas and concussion grenades was hurled. Little panic ensued as the people returned the cannisters of gas, accompanied by stones and fists.

....

Tear gas fell. Screams of outrage echoed across the waters. Rifle butts smashed into bodies to be answered by fists and feet. At least eight helicopters circled and roared overhead, unheard by those creating their own fury of sound. People jumped to water to relieve the burning tear gas. I saw soldiers thrown to ground. There were injured people on the rocks beneath the bridge. I heard fists striking flesh.

....

We formed our own line thirty feet from the Army. Soldiers in small groups left the wedge and ran to waiting helicopters for evacuation. As it grew dark, we built fires. Spotlights from choppers made the scene glaringly real.

When the last of the soldiers finally left in darkness, a great cheer went up from the crowd. Later, Army Lieutenant Colonel

Greg Mitchell, in charge of the invasion of Kahnawake, said, "The strong resistance surprised us. It was amazing the way they reacted, especially since we weren't at the Longhouse or a sacred place."

Dear Mr. Mitchell and Dear Canadians: Will you ever begin to understand the meaning of the soil beneath your very feet? From a grain of sand to a great mountain, all is sacred. Yesterday and tomorrow exist eternally upon this continent. We natives are the guardians of this sacred place.

Contemporary Life

The excerpts below come from a series of interviews, during which Laura Wittstock tells the story of her life as a Seneca woman. We learn in her narrative not only how Seneca culture is experienced today, but also how a Seneca woman perceives the tribe's position in history.

We Are All Members of a Family

Source: Jane Katz, editor, *Messengers of the Wind, Native American Women Tell Their Life Stories.* New York: Ballantine Books. 1995. pp. 110-120. Reprinted with permission of the author.

I was born on the Cattaraugus Seneca Reservation in upstate New York. We've been there for many hundreds of years, in permanent agricultural villages. Our tribe has stability, and a broad base. We call ourselves the Hodenosaunee, which means the Longhouse People. We are part of the Iroquois Confederacy, a political alliance which was set up many centuries ago to unify and protect the Six Nations.

We have the Great Law, originally recorded on wampum belts — the symbols are geometric shapes formed with shells, conveying complicated messages widely understood by the people. We are a multilingual people. I learned the Seneca language from my grandmother. I was part of a large extended family. I remember attending ceremonies. I remember funerals.

I'm from the Heron Clan. The clan is a sort of sisterhood. Clan members used to live together in a huge longhouse under the authority of the clan mother. A woman derived her clan name and status from her mother. A son brought his wife home to his mother's house....

....

Men and women were equals. Most marriages were long-term relationships. But the women were not dependent on the men — the same yoke was on both their necks. If they separated, it wasn't such a big deal. The woman remained with her clan, the man returned to his mother's home.

....

My great-grandmother Eliza Mohawk was a member of a medicine society. She made calls to patients in a little one-horse buggy; she cured illness; she delivered babies. My father told me that when he was nine months old — around 1899 — he contracted pneumonia. The local doctor said there was no hope for him. When Great-grandmother heard that, she took him to her home; she doctored him; and, he got well. Some people thought it was a miracle; some thought she used witchcraft....

....

Handsome Lake, preaching at a meeting, helped the Indians of New York State adapt to white customs. (New York State Library — Special Collections)

Through the generations, we experienced setbacks and devastations. Our institutions, developed over many thousands of years, were challenged. The formal parts of government are the ones that get kicked in the teeth. Europeans came to our territory, they'd find out who the head guy was, they'd bargain and make deals, there was corruption, and this weakened us. Treaties were broken, we lost much of the land, many Iroquois were removed to western reservations.

The Bureau of Indian Affairs made the people on our reservation jump through hoops. Schools tried to extinguish our languages. The churches were looking for souls, land and an economic base.

....

After World War II, returning Indian servicemen brought home non-Indian wives from overseas, and many moved into cities in search of economic prosperity. So that continued the separation from the Longhouse Religion....

....

My mother believed the annihilation of Indians was part of the national agenda. She collected clippings of Indians from all over the country who were being persecuted, their homelands were flooded, they were dying. She said if we were not vigilant, we'd disappear.

Events occurred in the fifties and sixties which led to the formation of the American Indian Movement. [AIM]...

....

It was the early seventies, there was an "Indian renaissance," and we were optimistic....

....

In 1972 AIM members organized "The Trail of Broken Treaties."

....

AIM delivered a 20 Point Program which called for formation of a commission to review treaty commitments and violations, restoration of 110 million acres of land, restoration of the rights of terminated tribes, abolition of the BIA [Bureau of Indian Affairs] and so on. AIM recast the relationship between the U.S. and Indian nations. In the past, the government had always set the agenda.

....

In meetings at the White House, we protested the system of colonial government blocking change on many reservations. We made it clear that this grassroots hoi polloi group known as AIM was a legitimate voice of Native people. We had a groundswell of support from Indians all over the United States, and we were heard.

....

If I have any spiritual belief, it is connected to the Longhouse Religion. Spiritually, we Iroquois are all members of a family. We have a strong link with our homeland. I can understand why "The Trail of Tears" was so painful for the Cherokee. They had to leave behind the graves of their ancestors. That was sacrilege. It tore them apart.

....

We believe that all living things are linked; death is a transition from one form of matter to another, a return to the earth you came from. It is not our purpose in life to question why things die, but rather to do well while we have the opportunity to do so.

I hold all of life sacred. Ideas are sacred, the collective wisdom that we poor humans, with our limited understanding of the universe, can leave as a legacy to our children. The essence of that legacy is to live a good life, while fulfilling our responsibility to our community. This is a universal theme that has survived many generations.

Suggested Further Reading

Calloway, Colin G., *The American Revolution in Indian Country, Crisis and Diversity in Native American Communities*, New York: Cambridge Univerity Press, 1995.

Graymont, Barbara, *The Iroquois in the American Revolution*, Syracuse, NY: Syracuse University Press, 1972.

Maxwell, James A., ed., *America's Fascinating Indian Heritage*. Pleasantville, NY: Readers Digest Association, 1978.

Seaver, James Everett, *A Narrative of the Life of Mrs. Mary Jemison*, New York: J.D. Bemis and Co., 1824.

Wallace, Anthony F. C., *The Death and Rebirth of the Seneca*, New York: ,Vintage, 1972.

Yellow Robe, Rosebud, *An Album of the American Indian*, New York: Franklin Watts, Inc., 1969.